Salvinia Molesta

Salvinia Molesta

POEMS BY VICTORIA CHANG

To: Julia
from: Mom
Hope you enjoy,
—Victoria

The University of Georgia Press   Athens and London

Published by the University of Georgia Press

Athens, Georgia 30602

www.ugapress.org

© 2008 by Victoria Chang

All rights reserved

Set in Minion Pro

by Graphic Composition, Inc., Bogart, Georgia

Printed and bound by Thomson-Shore

The paper in this book meets the guidelines for

permanence and durability of the Committee on

Production Guidelines for Book Longevity of the

Council on Library Resources.

Printed in the United States of America

12   11   10   09   08   P   5   4   3   2   1

Library of Congress Cataloging-in-Publication Data

Chang, Victoria M., 1970–

Salvinia molesta : poems / by Victoria Chang.

    p.   cm. — (The VQR poetry series)

ISBN-13: 978-0-8203-3176-8 (pbk. : alk. paper)

ISBN-10: 0-8203-3176-7 (pbk. : alk. paper)

I. Title.

PS3603.H3575 S25 2008

811'.6—dc22   2008025293

British Library Cataloging-in-Publication Data available

For Penny and Todd

The beauty of the world . . . has two edges, one of laughter, one of anguish, cutting the heart asunder.

—Virginia Woolf

Contents

Acknowledgments

Grateful acknowledgment is made to the editors of the following publications in which these poems have appeared or will appear, sometimes in different form:

Blackbird: "Jiang Qing," "Two Trains," "Girdling," and "After Hanging Mao Posters"; "Postmortem Examination on the Body of Clifford Baxter" and "Salvinia Molesta" in significantly different form

Columbia: A Journal of Literature & Art: "Newlywed Ghazal"

Gulf Coast: "Union" and parts of "Two Trains"

Kenyon Review: "Cardinal" and "Sparrows"

Michigan Quarterly Review: "Currency" and "Hanging Mao Posters"

Mipoesis: "Truth" and "Moon Guitar Lessons"

New England Review: "Professor's Lover" and "Ars Poetica as Bird-feeder and Hummingbird"

Paris Review: "How Much"

Ploughshares: "Spring Planting" and "Proof"

Salt Hill: "Seven Stages of Genocide" and "Ars Poetica as Dislocated Theater"

Shenandoah: "One More Than One"

Southwest Review: "Bindweeds"

New Republic: "Distribution"

Threepenny Review: "Desire," originally published as "The Guests" in significantly different form

Tin House: "Seven Infidelities"

Triquarterly: "Love Poem with Bicycles and a Hotel," originally published as "Litany for the Legion of Unrelated People," and "Mulberry Tree"

Virginia Quarterly Review: "Ode to Iris Chang"

Water~Stone: "February 28, 1947" and "At the Office Late"

*

"Distribution" appeared in the *2007 Poetry Calendar* (Alhambra Publishing).

"Proof" appeared in *Poetry Daily* (www.poems.com) and won the *Ploughshares* Cohen Award for best poem of the year.

"The Professor's Lover" appeared in *Verse Daily* (www.versedaily .com).

"Two Trains" also appeared online in *Born Magazine* (www.born magazine.org) in a different version.

*

I'd like to thank my family for their support. I would also like to thank all of my friends and mentors and the good and generous poets out there. In particular, I would like to thank those who have helped to make this book better or who have been supportive in the process— Rick Barot, G. C. Waldrep, Linda Gregerson, David Baker, James Longenbach, Michael Collier, Richard Siken, Brigit Pegeen Kelly, C. Dale Young, and Edward Hirsch. A special thanks to Ted Genoways, whose vision and rigor I deeply admire, and deep gratitude for believing in my work. A gracious thanks to the Warren Wilson MFA Program for Writers (and the Holden Minority Fellowship Program), the Bread Loaf Writers' Conference, the Kenyon Review Writers' Conference, and the Sewanee Writers' Conference, for their fellowship support, and where many of these poems were first written and/or worked on. Thanks to *Ploughshares* for the Cohen Award. Finally, thanks to all of the kind people at the University of Georgia Press.

Salvinia Molesta

I

Hanging Mao Posters

She unrolls each poster
one by one,

the thrush of paper drops,
splendor

each time as his forehead
opens to small eyebrows,

to a mole that stares at her
like an eye, to a nose

belled outward over lips—
the source of everything

right. Even the trees
take flight.

Sparrows

—During Mao's "Four Pests" campaign against four evils—
rats, flies, mosquitoes, and sparrows.

I want to pull one down, look into its eye—
    there would be a village,

thatch, megaphone, and the tops of fists.
    Stub of sun.

Villagers with pots and pans that banged.
    We still live in an italicized world.

Those trees by the ocean, the slanted ones,
    imply hands and knees.

Jiang Qing

—Mao Zedong's wife committed suicide while under house arrest for crimes related to the Cultural Revolution.

Now the fire is sick. My throat, hoarse
and husky. My throat cannot take swallowing,

everything too thick for my shrinking tube,
even a sigh, all my breaths are sighs now.

I used to speak so smoothly in pavilions, even
crows and clouds came down to hear. Now they

blame me for deaths, even for the rain. I think
it's the rain that kills with its endless dropping.

I want to lie with you again, your cheek on my neck,
to see the darkened canals of your mind, eyes that

lied to me. I want to cut down this paper city, ask
you to rebuild it in red, center it, to smear your lips

on mine, fasten your thoughts into my head. Here
is a hammer. Here are some nails. With each new

thought, your hand around my neck still indents
me. Soon the wind will overtake my shadow.

Seven Stages of Genocide

I am teal. You look seemingly bull.
Even the moon is looking for partialities—
it shines blue on a field, but soaks
a hummingbird in snow.

*

I am a Jew in my mother's nightgown.
You are a Gypsy who has a paper route.
And there are red-skinned locusts everywhere
that wait to rise.

*

A soldier called us a herd of ignorant sheep.
Then shear away our whispers,
make us feel your draft.

*

I have the snow's coolness.
Neighbors covered with hard black hairs
prick me and we do not trust each other.
They are the same as me.
Like footprints in snow, they hide
the color of the enemy.

*

The death lists are up. Next to me stands
the neighbor I hate and his rabid dog that foams
and foams. The barbed wire around us forces me
to catch his breath that smells like goose.

*

When they tire, they bury my neighbor from
the neck down and let the German shepherds at him.
How his fists must have tried to clench.

*

Near the covered ditches, only
an ocean keeps confessing
starfish to shore.

Ode to Iris Chang

1

Listen: I can almost hear
the sea galloping below.
The trail winds down

through the Douglas firs,
as the shadows of a brain might.
At this fencepost,

under buckeye trees,
nuts have eyes like those
of buck deer, as if mocking me.

Let me look at you
for a thousand days without
turning. Let me know

your posture the way roots know.
Why do your footsteps no longer
match the beating in my chest?

I can no longer hear your breathing,
just the rain that can't hold back
its falling. Why do you think

a hike will mute such melancholia?
Mat down "it happened"
to "don't worry"? I am adding

your steps upwards,
subtracting the wet trees.
I watch the hawk catch

the wind currents—
how strange to think it is free
within its entrapment.

You still cannot hear what I hear—
the hawk's wings opening
like newly sparked tinder.

2

"The Nanking Incident as I See It"

> —*Nakamura Akira, professor of history at Dokkyo University*

The Chinese ignored
the Japanese army's summons to
capitulate.

3
Why can't I be the girl
getting her cuticles pushed back?
Or the one who
ate the leaf and its shadow? How I love
the shadows more
than the leaves that take and take.
I have grown used
to working under two dusty suns. Let the florid
smell of human meat
make the birds come down. Let it turn
your sail and pull you in too.

4
And while the woman waited

for the bayonet to settle

in her, she dreamt that a Japanese

soldier had sewn it in there one night,
then tiptoed downstairs and kissed

his son on the forehead.
How his wife

had left a bowl of rice, seaweed, and
dried horse mackerel

on the kitchen table,

how the wife may have

felt something, but an ocean has
no teeth.

It just tongues and

tongues.

5
How

to trust humans.

How to trust the earth
        when all that is there is a

derivative of mud.

6

Easier than she had planned—
Reed's Sport Shop and its glass case of

        Civil War pistol replicas,

                under deer heads frozen in their shame.

7

Tall and slender, the revolver
        of her body,

and the Oldsmobile,

        her head fastened to the window,

                red dripping into tiny rafts

        of vinyl.

8

Some days the lawn
                        smells like molasses
and the angel trumpet breeze
                        blows at the perfect speed.
But today is not that day.
                        The sky sounds like rope twisting,
dark clouds braid each other.

I climb up the orchard ladder,

cut off the head of the tree,

saw each limb down.

Birds dive around me in alarm.

I work my way around

the branches, down the trunk,

until nothing but a stump remains.

When I'm finished, it doesn't

start raining, the bark doesn't peel off.

The angel trumpets raise

their drooping petals, no longer

able to stop the hundreds

of blues that scatter through

the gate. My body feels light.

When the wind blows in,

it takes everything but the trunk.

Cardinal

The cardinal's crest, crown of spark, of fire,
its body flitting

side to side, wings enjambing the air, Christ of
little bones,

fluttering against my car's side mirror, resting
briefly,

then attacking its own image again. I had meant
to be over there—

a worker laboring in a fish commune in Guizhou,
with skin

like a silver carp and hands cut like gills, pond silt
through my vessels,

feeding parts of haddock to hake, sea bream to
flounder, gathering duck feces

for feed, the fish humming in my walls at night.
I had meant to have my mother's hand

around my throat for being a girl or meant to beat
my own daughter

with a broom, all the mirrors I looked into,
reflections missing.

Proof

They say my great uncle read foreign books
in a mud house in Nanking,

plowed his twenty acres, listened to
rare birds, disregarded

the willow's *hush.* One day he knelt in the street,
sign around his neck

that said: *Traitor.* Little Red Book spread like wax
on his back, even

birds spun their heads around. He labored with
peasants, hands turned rough.

He must have had eyes like golden orbs.
One day he disappeared.

I am standing in the dirt in La Jolla, perpendicular
to the earth,

weeds exploding, rows and rows of berries, clouds
that reach and sever.

He is hanging from a mud house in Nanking,
perpendicular to the earth.

Our angles are equal, therefore we are parallel.

Then there must be two birds, two shores,
two deaths.

Bindweeds

What pleasure it must be
to see pulp bind into paper

and the water forced
in streams under

heavy cast-iron rollers that
press and press. In the end,

each fiber is invisible,
only it and

the papermaker know
it is there.

A Japanese historian
hunches over his desk,

prints characters on warm paper
about rising buildings,

new postures of steel,
invention of the rice cooker.

He leaves out the soldiers
who had paid a fee, obtained

a ticket and a condom,
who had been led to a space

partitioned with sheets—
a pillow, a tatami mat,

a Korean woman.
And a rusted needle

with droplets of drug 606
to induce abortion.

In the fields, wild bindweeds
spread over miles and

miles, their stems crawl
over the ground and

twine around everything,
their hard-coated seeds can

sprout even after fifty years,
some nights you can hear

them cracking open.

Two Trains

—Taiwan and China are one hundred miles apart.

A train leaves Nanking traveling
    at sixty miles an hour; another leaves

Guangzhou, traveling at forty miles an hour.
    Question: which train will be

farther from Nanking when the trains
    meet in the middle of a field?

Does it matter that the sister on the
    faster train is pulling seven children,

half-lost, half-mad? That they spend
    forty nights in the train, following

the trophies of a dying army? Or that
    the woman left my great aunt in

Nanking, half-turned face, with her
    kingdom of furniture?

Answer: when the trains meet, they will
    be the same distance from anywhere.

But one will be empty. And I'll never
    know how many fingers circled

throats, how a mind empties out within a
cinching rope, why she picked

the dark lake with its silver polish, with its
deranged rain. Each night a train

doesn't stop. It just blows its horn, and
we listen, entwine our cold blue feet.

Union

Red-lidded, I have been here for hours,
old books smell of wood with flattened

moths. Pictures of Chinese hung by
their tongues. Bodies heaped into one

another—a man's head, another's arms,
a woman's white legs. Munch's lovers

kissing so hard, their faces fatten into one.
My stack of dollar books, the cash register

opening like a tongue stuck out, the old
one-armed man at the desk, his glasses that

have begun to drowse—what it must be like
to hug him, how his one good arm and

my right one might circle our bodies, how
they might shiver, form a perfect set.

February 28, 1947

*—Thousands of Taiwanese protested the killing of an old
street peddler by a Kuomintang soldier. Protesters were
allegedly killed by troops from China.*

The school day ended early and it pleased my father,
how skillfully the sky ran across his skin.

His mother was rolling out dough at home. Sparrows,
splendor, steam out of windows from nearly

risen buns, or was it flame feathering out of windows,
blood washed up on streets or

on faces on bodies that ran through streets, making men
beautifully red, running towards home, towards

the smell of boiling cabbage? There were hundreds of
bodies, or thousands, or hundreds.

It had started with an old lady selling cigarettes on a road,
she wouldn't bargain, or she wouldn't turn

her money over, or she spat on his uniform, or they were
smuggled cigarettes, yes, there was blood, yes, he

struck her down with a revolver butt, as if one body
could be beaten in isolation.

Ars Poetica as Dislocated Theater

There is a cliff. There is a woman on the
edge of the cliff. Her arms open. The sun
and sky become larger. The wind needles into
her. The piano acquires a body, strings come
in on all speakers. When the cameras have
gone, the cliff goes on taking the wind and the
wind goes along its normal path. But where
am I now, having seen the cliff, the woman
on the edge, having heard the music and its
crescendoing feet? Having seen the two white
swans paddling in front of Mr. Darcy's house?

*

The high windows. The statues. The grand
staircase. The sound of horses. You, a man in
a blue coat and riding boots. I, in a cream
empire dress in a drawing room, stitching together
ribbons, listening to the birds recoiling outside.
In love with the pond, the swans, the English air,
the man. I wake the next morning, trying
to pretend. Pretending this life, this era,
with its skyscrapers, stucco, music that makes
cars vibrate, men pouring concrete and snipping
hedges into shapes of animals, pretending.

*

In the better. In the future. In the infinity pool
that becomes ocean. In the fire pit. I want
to stop. But I can't. Because there is no
other ending. Even the man on horseback
shoots down birds. Even his house has kept
soldiers. Even the girl stitching ribbons will
one day hang from the chandelier, imagining
a room without ribbons, wanting my desk,
bundles of pencils, small window, papers with
letters that almost touch each other, tea that spreads
its stain in the cup, and takes the form of a wing.

After Hanging Mao Posters

All night her mind prepared like a
tilled field—

not a thing missing but a lake that
glows

like a wolf's eye. Thighs, hair,
shrieks,

a toeless foot dragging itself.
The red

poppies open and close, like little
mouths.

Waiting to fill and empty out the
next

person with its scent. Something is
about

to. Something is always about
to.

II

Spring Planting

Today I plant bougainvillea and hyacinth. Tomorrow, crocus
and candied pansies.

I am gardening, but my mind is tilling. The crows enter my yard.
They remind me of ink slabs

Chinese calligraphers used—not until mixed with water did
their black ink breathe and broth.

Each morning, goat-hair brush in hand, they sat near willows,
against a dropping moon, drew

all they knew of mist, of hillocks, of lightening behind mulberries.
How strange to think that in just one stroke,

they left themselves on the page. Today, you call to say
you've found a new woman,

not a pretty one, but one like the kind of high-quality porcelain
that stands up to daily use.

You say the word *ring*. I drop my spade. Was it *rain* or *wing*?
No, I am wrong.

And the crow I hate descends on the gate, as if to say *poor fool*.
You tell me she is a heart surgeon.

I imagine her suturing thread into others, recording onto paper
the opening and closing of the heart.

The crow cries in couplets. I bend to pull out another row
of palsied phlox you had planted last spring.

The Professor's Lover

People shouting outside, people hitting
a white ball over a net with their fists, people
sitting under trees. Trees stayed separate as
elms, willows. Then they stippled everyone
with shadow and everything went to pieces.
Suddenly, the wind clubbed against me like
a clapboard. You heard. People do things.
People collide like sex. You told me what you
heard. I repeated his name quietly. I repeated
her name loudly. And his wife suddenly had no
name. She became a rusted knob on a house,
she watched them inside soaping each other,
holding each other, the water between them.

*

I woke up too late. Here I am at another
poetry reading. The beams above don't look
like stars. They are rotting wood beams.
Professor X opens and closes his mouth.
There's a light that halos around his head and
a podium he clutches like a drink. I am not
listening. I am thinking of what you just told me.
I am thinking of him again. And his wife. And
the child. There is often a child. I remember
one summer. We sat in the little wooden café.
He said: *I miss my wife.* I imagined him biting
a wife's neck, kissing her with his eyes closed.
And I stared into those fierce eyes.

*

This laundry room was just a laundry room.
Where clothes beat against each other.
But I missed it, always missed something,
always have to be told. A laundry room
is not just a laundry room. A man is not
just a man. A young female student is not
just a young female student. Who is up from
a night of dancing on wooden floors. Up from
too many colored drinks. She pulls the old
married professor into the laundry room, he
doesn't push her away, and she cleans his mouth
with her lips and tongue, and their bodies beat
into each other, fold, collapse.

*

In my dreams, a heart attacking itself.
In a new dream, the telephone had replaced
the heart and it rang and rang but I couldn't
pick it up. In class, I stared at her bare back
and knew that he had run his rough fingers
across it. Had cried in its crooked tunnels.
Her back, his tears, the garden where his wife
pulled up weeds each year, the porch, the chairs
rocking on the porch, perhaps all connected.
I stopped under the willows and watched
people come out from the high field, laughing,
looking for rooms to meet in. In my dreams,
people keep meeting, then switching.

*

Hairy limbs, two eyes, cicadas stick and
unstick, little figures ribboning the trees, shout
on all sides of this narrow Tennessee road.
It is anguish not to see them, to know that
at once, they can lower themselves onto me
and do what they want, kick me with their
legs, drop down on me. Go ahead, come down
from the thicket of trees and point your legs
at me. You will all die. But what is that
through the trunks? A white cross as large
as a farm house. Even the cicadas stop their
factioning. What have I done? I begin to see
the road's failure, the cicadas' failure, my failure.

*

If you look at my eyes, do you see two holes?
Do you want to put your fingers inside the
emptiness? I want to tell you what is in there,
tell you about the men that have passed through
my mind just this morning. See them. See
their hair between my fingers, twining. And
twining. Am I guilty if I stand behind the
window and look? If I only desire to bloody
my fist? If my mirror holds a thousand faces?
But there are still the dreams. The bazaar of men.
There are still the nights. This road. The
cross. The empty benches before the cross.
The cicadas that eventually must come down.

Seven Infidelities

This night—fog unstitches everything,
bodiless street lamps, charcoal men appear
and disappear. The sound of whipping
but nothing is touching. The wind blows
a man's trousers away from his legs. The man
looks in a storefront and the reflection looks
nothing like him.

*

After ten years. He must have known
her body, that she shaved up to
the thigh only. He spent five hours
at the gym each day, recruiting
his neck muscles, lifting river beds in sets,
as they flowed past her house, like muddy
curls. Where she stood every day to see
if he drove by.

*

A phone message that the new girl had
burned my favorite blue sweater. Imagine
the sweater, with its wristless arms,
illuminating her face. Later, the man
gave her a blue sweater. And I woke
in a new city with cable cars glued to

metal tracks, sparks from buses
like flashbulbs, a layer of fog, light
as breath on my body.

*

A woman on a tour squints behind
a velvet rope, at the family portrait,
Going to the Opera. I recognize her look—
the desire to be in that living room, under
the crease of light, closed in that dress
with a train. Soon to be tongued by
a Vanderbilt dressed in black.

*

A tall Asian man lives three doors down.
Married to a short Caucasian nurse.
No snow to mask the lamp post, flagless
mailboxes, trees held up by two wooden stakes.
I want rumors. Then add a rake merged with red
leaves, a snapping fire, rowanberries down from
a storm. A tall handsome Asian man. Good hair,
good shoes. Lifts open the shutters every time
I jog past in the snow.

*

A professor's wife passed her husband's
lover, stood against the pewter
of the ocean, smelled the saline of
her country, dove down into
the blank sheet, waxed a wave
with her fin, glided like paper under
boats, back to hydrogen, back to
oxygen, to half of nothing, nothing.

*

I want to make out with Professor X tonight,
the girl says. She's late to the last
barn dance of the last night of the conference.
The wood floors begin to shake as an
animal cage might. Somewhere in Asia,
houses fall into an ocean with all the people
bumping into sofas, colliding in the dark.

Moon Guitar Lessons

So many days she interrupted, without
her husband,

the gold-molared man. Her perfume fastened
to everything, red lips made

the roses look pale. I went out into
the dark well

of snow that flung itself at the window, arctic
wind turned my fingers into wood.

I left Uncle Li and the woman in the kitchen,
which smelled of gently

braised bok choy, beef as fragrant as lavender.
And I never noticed the scent

of sex, two burning cigarettes in the tray, the year
she never came back.

Because I didn't know what it was like to be
fire, because

I couldn't imagine all that happened behind
drapes, because I couldn't yet see

how light could hit a red bird and scatter
in a thousand different directions.

Truth

Come in your handfuls, soothing
scents, your small

canisters, through the accordion
mirror, past the ax

that may have swung, the professor
shoveling his driveway,

past the young girl who may have
shared his

toothbrush just once, under a nickel or
brass or bronze moon,

or just twice under a convex mirror—
did they or not?

Answer me. Someone. I just want
to know, to near, to be

shown, there—a place where sinuous-
steel springs mean

just that, where there are no fabric options,
just *yes, I cheated*

on the problem set. You are a problem
set, over me,

under me, on me, because there are
at least two of you,

sometimes seventy-two million of you.
One: bleached bone,

two: elliptically green, three:
arsenic-laced,

four: my head down a sink, rippling,
digging, leaving

my thumbprints on anything not gray.
Stop putting

your hands on me. Make me taste
salt or light.

Mulberry Tree

—Van Gogh

Here is the forest
where he leaned
against trees to see

if they would hold him or
eat him.
Near the asylum

where his ceiling glittered
like an electric fence.
Where nightly he

entered the crack
in the wall.
Where a wren flew

backwards into a field
of bald trees.
Where he scarred

canvas with yellow
tentacles
so they could be tongued.

Here is a train
that whines with
hurt. Where nothing

touches on purpose—
the girl's yellow handbag
against the blackness

of a man's leather coat.
Where nothing is
transparent—a man's

sunglasses, the checker-
board of a
houndstooth blazer.

Here is a train
holding a girl
dying from sarcoma.

Where the damaged
are screened.
Where I glare at the girl

for her talk. Her look.
Her ugly shoes.
Where I can't hear

the final drop of her neck.
Where I can't see
the tree

that burns and burns,
but never catches
on fire.

Newlywed Ghazal

My mother suggests fava beans, though their flesh
is hard to reach—first a thin sheath, a second of fleshier

skin. Next, the cured tofu, to be sliced into rods,
a layer of darker brown, bound by lighter flesh.

No matter how I try, I can't get the pieces as small
as hers; mine always glare at me like the eyeballs of fish.

Even without looking down, she can slice pork into
even strips, but my knife slides under my flesh.

Slips of onion laugh and laugh as I rub my eyes. Under
each sliver lies more and more secrets that make me flush.

I wonder why she never said to stop peeling, stop my
search for another's heart, never told me that flashing

a smile while frying would be enough, would fill
the shadows in a marriage. She still bundles flesh-

pink orchids for the table. My father waits.
She still uses onions each day, always ready in a flash.

Love Poem with Peanut Shells

Now I am in the warm oil of your mouth,
comfortably sleeping in your throat. We build
with flagstone, shop for sconces and radiance.
Your large hands bundle and stack wood into walls.
You digest my shape, unlit layer, lung. Light
begins here, where we are one decimal point, where
I stand with a cool blue hat that covers my eyes,
red shoes that drop anchor. Where we sit in bars
with peanut shells with Mikes and Leroys and Toms.
Where you counsel me on lips and throat. Where
you love the hiss of my atom. Where the ocean is zero
miles from everywhere. Here, madness has no map.
Here, God is abridged. O to be loved this way.
To have lips that bear fruit. To be cancelled.

Little Gem

You're on your hands and knees,
             planting a magnolia tree,
a "little gem,"
             grinning up at me,
                          asking which side
should face the street:
             even a perfect tree is   wayward.

*

The Bundt cake's bell draws me
             back in,
the message on the computer—
             Chris is survived
                          by his wife, Lynn,
his children Sydney and Evan,
             his parents, and his brother.   Still,

*

beneath each layer lies
             another and another
until a maze
             of brittle brambles cross
                          and grow, the way
our fig vine nails
             its leaves onto the wall with   sap,

*

crisscrosses like something
        chased.
I've sat for hours wondering if
        I could see it
                spiral and splay, but
it moves when I turn my back.
        They say the car   accident

*

was his fault—vodka. That it happened
        at 3 a.m. while his wife was
baking a Bundt cake,
        the sides of the spindles pecking
                against the tin, grinding its
bone against metal. They say
        there was a younger   woman

*

at the office with freckles
        on her chest.
That he regularly kissed her in the
        underground
                parking lot, tore
her blouse, as yellow batter might
        open itself up,   stitch

*

itself back up and unstitch over and
       over.
They say he broke his legs, arms,
       and back, that
          the heart split itself,
that there was a suction sound as
       the halves   unlocked.

*

Your hands look like claws
       covered with dirt.
I have them. I covet them. I wonder
       if I can ever
          truly have them, ever
uncover the thorns that may
       constellate underneath your   palm.

Ars Poetica as Birdfeeder and Hummingbird

All winter I watched the empty feeder
and the God light pummel

its stained glass in a sieve. No
hummingbirds, no

humorous little body with a tent stake
as a nose.

Look, little bird, how do you know, how
do you know

your brilliance is what I seek? The way
you lance a honeysuckle's

heart, take the blood in your bill. I wish
I knew how to punch

a center, inch in and in, lance something
to death, that flowers and

flowers light. You in your array of vibrating
attire. I am not

a weed, I need your praise to survive.
The field will consume me.

The field has chosen sides. The field is
not hungry for the middling.

How I hate the field and what it sees, its
teeth digging out the ochre

of mediocre, what's left but medi—a non,
a nothing, no-one.

O tiny bird—medicate me, convulse me,
punch holes in me so

some of my light leaks out.

Love Poem with Bicycles and a Hotel

The bike race starts and the starting makes me disappear again.
Men in spandex, corporate logos, spokes, wheels,
so many sponsors—hearing aids, television channels.
So much spandex. So many autographs that
never seem to fix anything.

*

You drink from your water bottle up the first climb. I am not scared.
I am wild with pride. Because I know you,
the man in the bike race. I woke up knowing you.
But I am not you. In my dream, I am standing on the edge
of a bridge. Hundreds of people clap
when I jump off. I am not lit up.

*

They go in circles for five laps so fast they become one man.
I'm afraid to yell your name.
You might think you're human and crash.
The sound of my voice means I must be alive.

*

I enter the hotel lobby, thousands of people circle booths.
Plastic nametags around necks: Nancy Dell, Jim Smith.
Little bags stuffed with white papers on the environment.
I am a hotel chair, row 67, 73 in. Counting from the left.
The Flamingo Room. Do they know about the others across
the road? Splitting the air on their carbon-fiber machines.

*

I am outside again. Their legs show signs of work. Some have
pulled out. Some need stitches that will leak.
Sweaty, they finish. They shower. They sleep.
Wake up, clip in, ride for six hours. It gets dark. It gets light.
It gets dark again. Then light.

*

The people in the hotel have long since returned to their rooms.
In another city. Train. Casket. I know what I must do—
try to hear the newspaper on the porch, hear the sprinkler
on a rainy morning, hear your breathing in mine.

Desire

A space must be maintained or desire ends.
—Anne Carson

The sun applies itself and bends, tries to debut
on my ankle, tries to copyright my body.
Because of you I let the sun iron my back until
it combusts. I let the waves swindle my body,
enter all of its cavities. I let the airplane in the
sky disappear, just as the white clothes on the
line become the wind. It is not space I desire,
but a dying, as crows might stalk the sky, bankrupt
air, content in their coming and going, content
in their similar blackness, in how their blackness
resembles every shadow; as clothes in a dryer in
a laundromat at 3 a.m. might finally stop
unclenching and accept their entanglement.

Love Poem as Eye Examination

The room became a raven until a white fire lit
the wall. The doctor's breath alarmed

and I was suddenly inside this bird, looking out
of its eye. O doctor,

why do you set traps, map out what I see,
cage my broken eyes,

make clear the branch that was fire, the geese
that were windmills rotating?

Which is better: *one or two, three or four?* What if
I don't need choices?

What if I can't see the letters—the P always looks
like an F. Or the F is

really a P that has opened its floodgates. What if
I am the F and my river never thins?

If there isn't a last row, a disappearance?
Then I want his salt in my eye,

his hand that perforates the gate with paint, that
nails cabinets in our garage, that joins

our scavenged bodies and pulls them through
the flaming flue.

III

Currency

The Federal Reserve adjusts, raises,
lowers, and we follow, predictably,

to purchase the milk or to hold off
on the love seat. *In God We Trust*

labels the backs of bills to reveal
that bills are backed by faith,

while we war and search pockets for
more. Days never change tempo,

a metronome stuck on moderato,
even on our last day, when flies

seem to crawl and sparrows suspend
in air. Each day a thirsty dog and

an old man wander the streets, no
longer in season, or having currency,

they leave the same smell behind—
of resin, of garbage, that near-death

odor—how easily we exchange them,
how easily we create more.

At the Office Late

The wind rises. The building lets in high-pitched trills
like the sound of sparrows trapped.

I am inside, at the center of this giant birdhouse, big as an
upstate hotel.

Through the offices, flocks dive and skitter for mealworms
at my feet, whistle

in parabola, two trumpeter swans atop a small lake,
a snowy owl on a ledge.

But all of this must end, the puffins gone, the thrumming
of wings, gone, the humming

gone, and everything they bring with them—yews,
groomed ponds, sound of ram hooves,

of horn, gone. Nothing left here but these numbers,
thousands of them,

the Herman Miller chair, papers like resting tombstones.
But the owl, still here, looking

through its lens into each office, if only we had such vision.
It's not just the fall I seek, but the whole of it—

the twilight before disgrace, the surprise of seeing
a once brilliant creature in a storm's

carousel, and the temporary stillness of the water.

Ars Poetica as Corporation and Canary

Now I see the thin body of glass,
the corpus for what it is,

a breathing corpse—as the moon
confesses light

from the sun, but can never truly
have it. I am

a corporation, a for-profit stock one.
A stout fist on a table.

I want to generate something but
I don't want

to spend anything. I have read,
understood, and disagree

with everything. But I am authorized
to execute on nothing.

I have received a copy of this
agreement in the rain.

The rain is always looking for a way
into my mouth.

My body holds pushpins. This one is
yellow. This one red.

They tack memorandums to my
skin. That cover my sores.

That cover the canaries that lie
beneath, little birds that

fly into the window, fly farther and
fluster, that fly back into

the window. The window clarifies.
The building bunts

the birds. The building envelopes
the birds.

The window loves me. I love the
building. I loathe the building.

The building is a headquarters that holds
me, that I return to, that

I report to. And I can't see myself
on the glass until it's too late.

Collision

*—Clifford Baxter was a former Enron executive who
committed suicide.*

1

Year after year, he added zeroes with perfect
curves, charred numbers, dove into a ledger
in which he missed the green lines. On a
rainy day, he stood under a peach tree, he was
the only one out, and the harder it rained,
the more dirty he must have felt. They
found him in Sugar Land, bullet hole in his head,
scribbled note. How he must have pulled the
trigger halfway, released it, pulled it again, how
it must have felt like the space between
dreaming and waking. How it must have
sounded like a child's shriek from inside a well.

2

In the hundreds, on the mended gate, past
the mulch and meadowsweet, bodies of all
wings with red eyes, past the second summer,
second winter, third summer, third winter.
White nymphs dive, search for tree roots,
feed on sap, gnaw nodes for seventeen years,
swelling and swelling, not bursting, but nearly so.
How do they count to seventeen? How do
they know when to bloom, rise, break out
with wings, mate, burrow new eggs into
tree branches, die weeks later, new nymphs
dripping down into soil, repeating the cycle.

3

Plastic 3-D glasses, *Dial M for Murder,* me
stumbling into the theater, I only wanted 3-D—
her hand reaching at my hair, not gleaming
scissors, the nylon nearly around my neck,
not hers. I wanted her perfect face, curls,
the way she said, *Tony,* as if everything were
about to come out but couldn't—the hidden
letter, sex. Now, seventeen years later, I see
her affair with the boyfriend, red dress, whiskey,
her back rubbing against a brick wall, welling
spaghetti sauce. After, the boyfriend on her
bed eating a drumstick, watching *I Love Lucy.*

4

The men are pressing stone onto a gate,
they are singing to a song on the radio from
the 1950s, cicadas can't make out the words
so they buzz louder. A boy watches *Dial M
for Murder* during a Hitchcock marathon.
He puts on an old pair of 3-D glasses but the
bodies only become darker. A mother holds
a wooden spoon, the red sauce swells, a man sits
upstairs, a dog gnaws on a dead bone. The man
is sweating, the gun is rusting. The police are
coming. He looks down at them. And at
the peaches in the trees that look like ears.

Distribution

It might be anything: cowries, eggs, pigs, hoes.
In Bangalore, they use dry fruit, in Iceland,

dried fish—a horseshoe for one fish, a pair
of woman's shoes for three, casket of butter for

one hundred twenty. The paper dollar on my desk
has value because we think it does.

The antelope against the barren hills is running
across the field because we think it is.

Satellites hang in space to spy on the French man
tilling his field, the Russian man filling jam jars

with florets of fruit, the Chinese man opening
his palm of starfish. A science experiment gone

according to plan, the laboratory—us. The problem:
one earth, one football field, one home

in the suburbs, too many of us. What if there is not
enough grass to trample, and the rain never cleans

the streets, just pushes things around, like a broom
sweeping in a room with no door?

Epistles

—Clifford Baxter

Dear Past,

I am muzzled by your gaze, your wheeze
that slants, as light might enter through a
window, making a table's legs look longer.
You are a list that I find with no letters.
You are an arm hung over my shoulder.
You are a sigh that scrapes my neck. I feed you
as I feed gulls—with my fists. There is no present.
Only You.

*

Dear Winter,

The first frost on the porch. But it still
feels hot. On this day, I shut all the windows
because I know there will be a death.
In this darkened room, shapes still curve up—
the chin of the child, the bottom of the
whiskey glass: so much yet untouched.

*

Dear Finch,

Death finch. Finch, I love you.
Finch, you lynch me. *Come with me* you call.
Your voice bevels my nights and I toss and toss
without a turn. Until I decide to go with you.
My small bag, a blanket in hand. But you have departed.
I can still hear your heart, how it sounds so much
like a baby's rapid beat.

*

Dear Crow,

Behind you two trees. I've killed you but
you return to peck at my stale seeds.
I miss your double call. I wish
I too could live with no consequence.
I'd love to fly in blackness from elder
to willow and back again. I'd love how
everything would scatter under the lawn.
I'd love how there would be no such thing as
property. Just worms that wrestle and wrestle
in my throat.

*

Dear Hill,

I can hear your mud whimpering. I slip when
I walk up. I can't bear to walk in a straight line.
If I rub my eyes I can see my mother's fingers
in my hair again. I'm looking for the field
where we played Wiffle ball next to cows, where
we couldn't yet see the marks of the bird's beak
on the trunk. Where the trunk restored itself.
Where the trunk cleaned itself up.

*

Dear Sparrow,

Yellow-breasted bird, resting on this knobbed
branch that hardly holds your orthogonals,
diagonals. You, you knight in a net of yellow,
who pawns wind, borrows light, knows both
pleasure and *loss.* O little Coronet, how do you
seize and share the sunflower? Sequence your song
while stunning the worm? In your world
there is only *catch,* no *caught.*

*

Dear Body,

My love for you is conditional. I have overfed you and
now you are eating me. This is why. This is why
I have led you into the forest. Into the mist. I promise
to put a hood over your head. I promise to bring
no dogs. I promise that you will hear oblivion.
And its fire will finally soothe you by erasing you.

*

Dear Ocean,

Above you, gulls that wait to take. Clouds fragment
everything. I wade a little and watch people leaving
behind names in sand. Soon they too will be gone.
Because that is the grammar of the ocean.

*

Dear Carol,

How did you know that this earth
could not contain my velocity? That I am
a hummingbird resting on a fountain, my
nose in spilling water. That without
the madness of my wings I am nothing.
That in a moment I won't be here.

How Much

A boy drowns in a lake. Another opens
his head against a steering wheel. Another
goes downtown. Into a board room. Into
leveraged buyouts. Into Italian shoes.
Into spearheading something. *Hi, you've reached
Victoria Chang. I'm not at my desk right now.
Please leave a message at the beep.* Never mind
the kickbacks, passing the sound barrier in
the Concorde, its hypodermic body. How much
mahogany we all had. Cheese stabbed with
sticks our teeth tugged on. How many drivers
in black cars we said *Happy Valentine's Day* to.

*

Each morning, I put on those shoes, legs,
nylons, sex, black briefs with texts. Each
dusk, there were martinis, starters, soup and
salad, main meal, dessert on trays, coffee in
thimbles, men scraping bread crumbs off a
table. Business models. Pigeons on ledges
I watched. Dimmed rooms with white
screens, a man with a pointer. No one stops
him. Someone make him stop. My watch gets
tired from looking up at me. The next table is
once again pioneering something. I can shake
a hundred hands in an hour. Watch me.

*

$13 a share. The man on the phone line
has a rope in his throat. The closing price is
rouged. We can believe in God again. The banks
are full. The streets are hungover. The man on
my left is rich. The man on my right is a month
from dead. The champagne ditches its bottle.
The London air free-falls in the hotel room.
There are plates of carved fruit. New York is
cheering through the phone. Heaven must
be this way. Tomorrow, Germany. Then Paris.
*Hello. Goodbye. Where's the bathroom? I don't
understand. I am lost. How much?*

*

A man carrying a tray of sandwiches.
A woman on a cell phone. The doorman
on California Street. The cable car driver.
No one knows how beautiful the check
looks in my wallet. $94 million. Tomorrow,
$106 million. From: iv Drip. To: Bob
Dell. From: Ivy hiccupping up a wall.
To: John Hedge. Everyone is drunk today.
Everyone is preparing for sex today. Little
turquoise boxes with white ribbon are hand-
delivered around town today. The smell of
beef is powerful. The cemeteries are still full.

*

The first sound of the stitched ball finding
its glove. The corporate seats. The Samsung.
The Solectron. The Synopsys. The Pitch.
Positioning. Presentations. Summer that
can't stop its inverting. The cartoon ball
under the cartoon hats that keep moving.
One, Two, Three, the crowd shouts. Some day
the big screen will dangle in rust. The headless
field will become untethered. Some day
the last rain will dry on the sleeping dog.
Somewhere in a kitchen, a mother will watch
the last piece of beef fall off a bone.

Anagrams (of Clifford Baxter's Suicide Note)

If he says, *I am sorry,* then why
do the words so easily become *Am I sorry?*

And how *I can't go on* so simply turns into
a con got in or

contagion, a disease that spreads and spreads
across the garden,

among the dead bones, into
any body with cells.

He writes he has always tried to *do
the right thing,*

then why does it become *dig, then
high trot*—somewhere

between a walk and a run. Who says one
foot must always be on this earth?

When trotting fast, hunting something or
being hunted,

all feet are momentarily off the ground
at once, like a star.

He must have *tried* to make things right,
but just got *tired.*

In the end, *Carol* might turn
into *coral*—

the pink kind under the sea, the kind that
holds its shape in any tide.

In the end, *Cliff* just turns into
cliff—

a high steep or overhanging face of
any rock.

October

Now the porches are empty.
They are motionless. They are worthless.

Their lights quiver.

On one, four pumpkins frozen in misfortune,
their grimaces carved.

Only one untroubled, horned grin of a baby.

Last night, each masked boy looked inside
his bag after the candy fell.

As if looking would change the outcome.

Now, without listeners, between wind,
the pumpkins say: *I want to die.*

They are like humans.
They rot from the inside out.

Postmortem Examination on the Body of Clifford Baxter

The body received in blue workout pants,
short-sleeved blue T-shirt, brief-style underwear.

Those unlucky clothes that might have
seen the moon in June.

But they contain a body,
$\qquad\qquad$ stiff as a canoe.

*

The head is deformed due to the bullet into
the right temporal area.

O to be born a bullet, mute for
most of its life,

One quick explosive motion
$\qquad\qquad\qquad$ and pieces stray away,
search for bodies to embed in,

to make things beyond recognition.

*

An abrasion on the left hand and base of second digit.
How the fingers can never again point—

    they are pointless,

permanent in disgrace, no longer able to insist,
to begin a list,

    to buttress a kiss.

    *

Small shards of glass on a shirt,
but nothing nearby broken.

The ring missing.

The body received without the hands
bagged. Even the dead must be contained.

Earlier a starling sat on a fence,
said nothing.

"One More Than One"

—Eva Hesse, sculptor, died of a brain tumor at the age of thirty-four.

In this world, we have no use
for such a thing—brick-like lintel

fastened to a wall. Two concave
holes through the block. Holes emitting

two cords that dangle to the floor.
The room is white and icy.

In this world, we have use for
each lobe. Little frontal one,

where intellect and creative thought
live together, losable

at once, in one moment. There are over
120 different types of brain tumors,

they grow in stealth, drinking cups of
light and water, of ambition.

Here, the two hollow holes stare back
as if to say, on their side is life, and

in this gallery, with its whirr of used air,
the dying. Once, she said:

Life doesn't last, art doesn't last, it doesn't matter.

The cords, then? As if she already knew.
The twin ropes are limp, they twist, tease,

distract . . . as if to say, *Come, climb in,*
it is cooler in here—no weather fronts,

no filthy doves that tempt, no tangled brain matter,
just stars that grow like hair.

Salvinia Molesta

—Known as the world's worst weed, it lives in water and doubles its numbers every two days, eventually becoming a continuous green mat over the water surface.

1

How do they grow, spread and sickle
outward and away?

Their rings climb upward too, into
chains,

and downward underwater,
their filamentous fronds twist

in egg-shaped sporocarps.
Miles and miles of them diving and

dividing. Eventually, they block
sunlight from everything below and

fish burn in hunger and scum.

2

Name: Frank P. Quattrone.
Dubbed: *God's banker.*

As if God too needed
a portfolio adjustment.

3

I often watched him through the glass in his office,

he liked speakerphone—talked to walls, his desk,

wisterias, and

    blood grass outside.

His striped shirt with the good seams.

      Sometimes he picked up the putter

while talking. What patience he had putting
the pocked ball into the machine over and over.

And the moustache that hung there
          without discipline,

    it moved in concert with the mouth,
    clenching and unclenching, but

      was slightly off.

    A truth lay beneath it.

4

When did honeysuckles
and hummingbirds
accrue, worms sew

into sod, sassafras
recover from its
transplanting?

When did snails
sex, fill a shell?
When did I stop

seeing the shell, stop
believing the heart
that must exist?

5
My tongue on two-pound lobster,

porcini mushrooms, pear onions, lardoons.

My body soaking in tubs that filled in sixty seconds.

My hands around six irons, forged metal
meant to strike a small ball.

How I loved rotating my body on an axis

and the shock of a stricken ball.

People passing the sound barrier
in the Concorde,
delta-winged body,
a quiver
that moved so fast over

a couple
      making love on
            a boat
          that they looked
           like a
           cross.

6

There was an e-mail.
A sweeping of files.

A weeping with his wife.

And a human desire to name it:
obstruction of justice, witness tampering.

What is justice but that which just is
a majority, logic, divine authority.

People said:

Impossible,
possible,
possibly impossible,
impossibly possible.

7

I wanted a blue shirt like his.

I wanted objects but not their shadows.

I wanted a house
with a vellum of lawn, blades

and weeds thrown onto the earth.

What if what had happened could
happen again?

What if we are all innumerable

plants that float and circle?
That pour and expand as quietly as sun.

8
How well this is understood
elsewhere: the way a lake

makes passages for orange fish,
but takes in lightening and

shatters it; the way a pair
of wings as soft

as a child's palm fasten
to a bird's beak meant for

tearing and jewelling.

9
When the court adjourns and he is free,

       he becomes a magpie in Iberia.

   Let me be frank.

          Maybe I have been wrong all along.

Maybe we live in incomplete sentences.

Maybe there are no verbs—*did, did not.*

Just nouns:

fire,

wind,

weed,

end.

Girdling

—Nine women claim a baby boy in Sri Lanka.

One will eventually win, perhaps the loudest or
the one with a sack

of rupees. The boy will grow up and wonder
about the other eight

who quarreled over him. He will wonder about
the one who threatened to

kill herself. He will move through life, deeper
and deeper into the trees,

until suddenly, a clearing—a single ficus
in the center of a field,

its roots wrapping tightly around the trunk,
a slow choking of itself.

The wind will pause around the damaged trunk,
the way it considers

a splintered fence. The boy will pause.
He will bend down, touch

the root's collar, cut just outside of it, angle
his knife down and away.

He will go from tree to tree, lit by the light
of nine moons.

He will do this until the earth's roots flurry out
and untangle themselves.

Notes

The opening epigraph is from Virginia Woolf's *A Room of One's Own.*

"Ode to Iris Chang" refers to a Chinese American author who wrote a highly debated book on the December 1937 invasion of the Chinese city Nanking by the Japanese army. Within weeks of that conflict, some say more than 300,000 Chinese civilians and soldiers were raped, tortured, and murdered. Iris Chang committed suicide in 2004. "The Nanking Incident as I See It" is quoted from http://www.jiyuu-shikan.org/nanjing/nak.html.

"The Professor's Lover" was inspired by Richard Siken's "Unfinished Duet" in *Crush.*

"Newlywed Ghazal" was inspired by Suji Kwock Kim's "Monologue of an Onion" in *Notes from the Divided Country.*

"Ars Poetica as Birdfeeder and Hummingbird" is conversing with Louise Glück's poem "Witchgrass" in *Wild Iris,* in particular, her lines: "I don't need your praise / to survive" and "I will constitute the field."

The epigraph to "Desire" comes from Anne Carson's *Eros the Bittersweet.*

The idea behind "Anagrams (of Clifford Baxter's Suicide Note)" was inspired by Peter Pereira's "Annagrammer" in *What's Written on the Body.*

The italicized portions of "Postmortem Examination on the Body of Clifford Baxter" are from the coroner's report in slightly altered form. One fact has been changed from "fifth digit" to "second digit." Joye M. Carter, Office of the Medical Examiner of Harris County, www .whatreallyhappened.com/Autopsy_Pg1.jpg.

"One More Than One" refers to the title of Eva Hesse's sculpture.

Frank Quattrone, referred to in "Salvinia Molesta," is a former investment banker and prior boss who was accused of obstruction of justice in 2003 but eventually cleared of charges. The e-mail is a reference to several e-mails related to Credit Suisse First Boston's document retention policies, mentioned during legal proceedings. Information about *Salvinia molesta* comes from the U.S. Geological Survey: http:// salvinia.er.usgs.gov/html/comparison.html.